Start Reading
AND WRITING

What's in the Sky?

Ian Smith

QED Publishing

Copyright © QED Publishing 2004

First published in the UK in 2004 by
QED Publishing
A Quarto Group Company
226 City Road
London, EC1V 2TT

www.qed-publishing.co.uk

A Catalogue record for this book is available from the British Library.

ISBN 1 84538 321 4

Written by Ian Smith
Designed by Zeta Jones
Editor Hannah Ray
Picture Researcher Joanne Beardwell
Illustrated by Chris Davidson

Series Consultant Anne Faundez
Creative Director Louise Morley
Editorial Manager Jean Coppendale

Printed and bound in China

Picture credits

Key: t = top, b = bottom, m = middle, c = centre, l = left, r = right

NASA/20b, 21b, 22m; **Corbis**/Raymon Gehman 4 /Dennis Scott 20t;
Getty Images/Steve Bloom 15.

Contents

The Sun

Imagine a bonfire so hot that you could warm your hands on it while standing on the other side of the street.

Now imagine something so hot that it warms your hands from MILLIONS of kilometres away! That's how hot the Sun is to us on Earth.

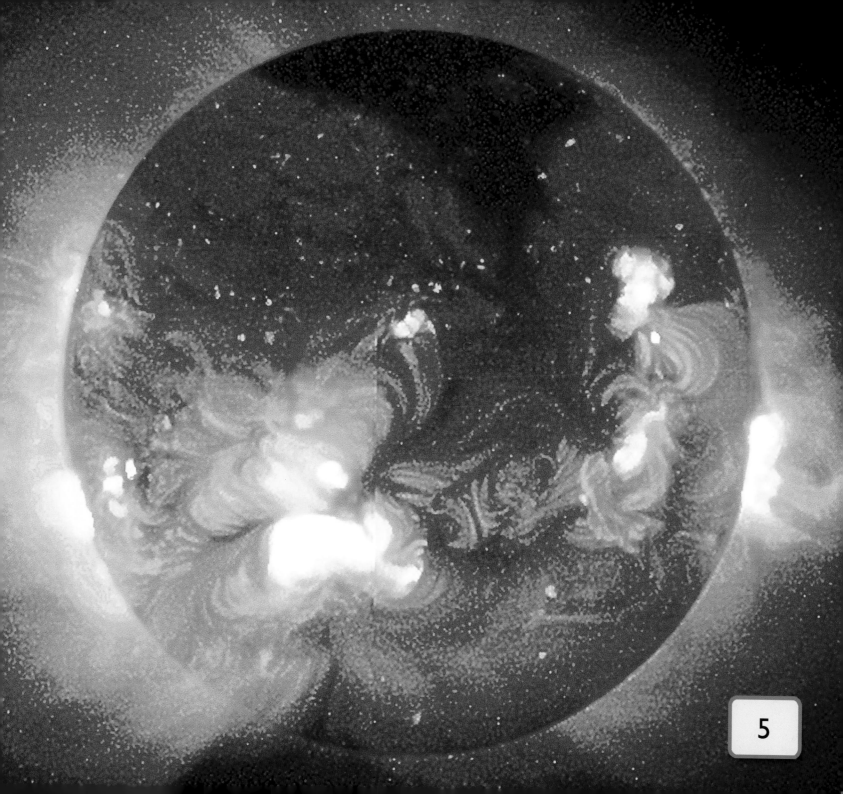

The Earth

To an **astronaut** looking down from space, our Earth looks like a huge ball.

The Earth spins round all the time, like a giant top. It takes a day and a night to spin the whole way round.

Day and night

The side of the Earth that faces the Sun has daytime. The side that turns away from the Sun has night-time.

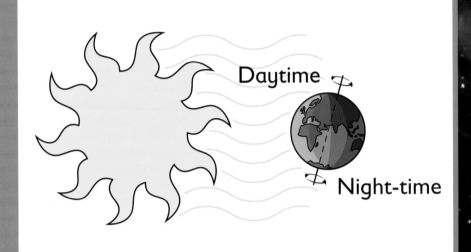

Daytime

Night-time

As it spins, the Earth also travels around the Sun. The Earth takes a year to move all the way round the Sun. That's from one birthday to the next!

Weather

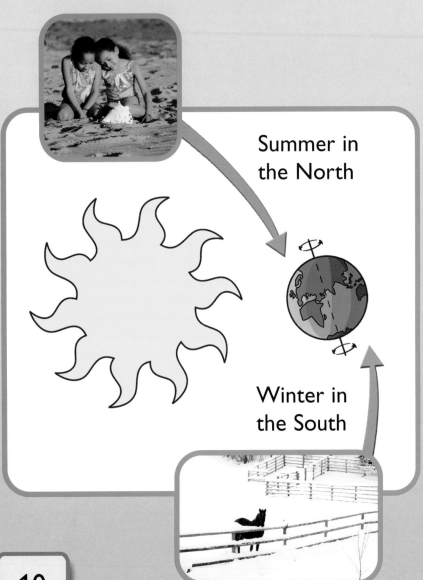

Summer in the North

Winter in the South

The part of the Earth that is leaning towards the Sun has warm weather.

The part of the Earth that is leaning away from the Sun has cold weather.

That's why it's cold in winter and hot in summer.

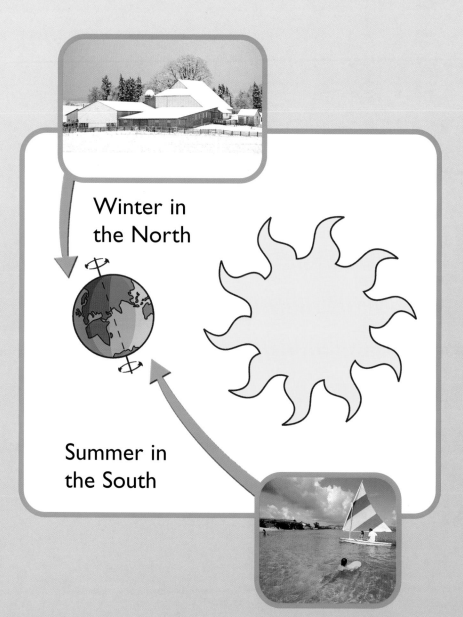

Winter in
the North

Summer in
the South

When it is winter in one part of the Earth, it is summer in another.

While children in Britain enjoy the snow, in Australia they are cooling off on the beach!

The Earth seen from the surface of the Moon.

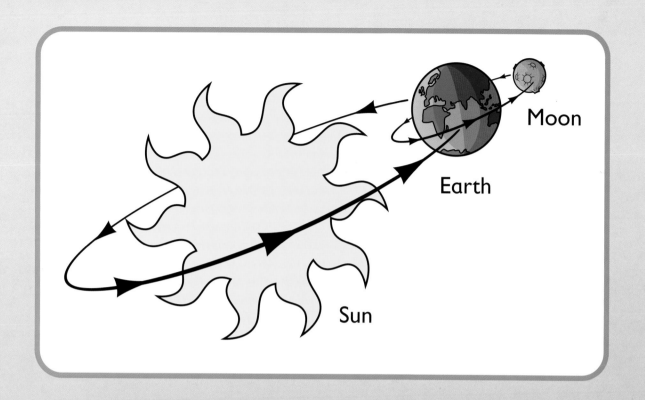

Moon

Earth

Sun

The sky is a very busy place! As the
Earth moves slowly around the Sun,
the Moon moves around the Earth.
But it goes much faster. It takes the
Moon only about a month to go all
the way around the Earth.

The Moon has no heat or light of its own. It **reflects** the light of the Sun.

New Moon

A 'New Moon' is nearly all in shadow.

Full Moon

A 'Full Moon' is nearly all lit up by the Sun.

The Moon seems to be a different shape each night that you look at it.

The Stars

What else do you see when you look up into the sky at night? You can see lots of stars twinkling.

These stars are very far away from us. They are even further away from us than the Sun. That's why they look so small and don't seem as bright as the Sun.

17

The Planets

Some of the brightest lights that we can see in the sky at night are called planets. The Earth is a planet, and there are eight other planets. The other planets are called Mercury, Venus, Mars, Jupiter, Saturn, Uranus, Neptune and Pluto. All the planets move around the Sun.

Jupiter

Mars

Earth

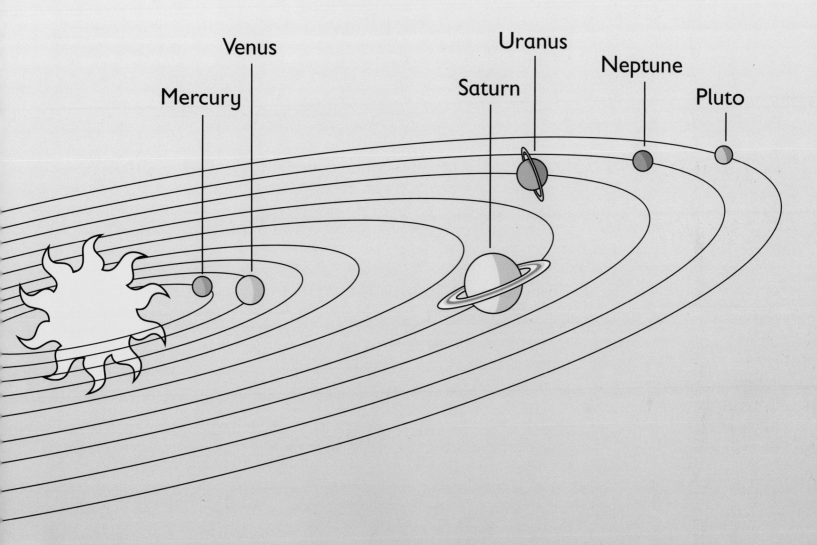

Venus

Uranus

Mercury

Saturn

Neptune

Pluto

Astronomers are also discovering more and more planet-like objects called **planetoids**. Some of the planetoids are even further from the Sun than Pluto.

The planets that are nearest the Sun are Mercury, Venus, Earth and Mars.

Mercury is the closest planet to the Sun and takes only **88** days to go right around it.

Mercury

Jupiter

Jupiter, Saturn, Uranus, Neptune and Pluto are very far away from the Sun. They circle the Sun very slowly.

If you lived on Neptune, you would have to wait 165 years for your birthday to come round!

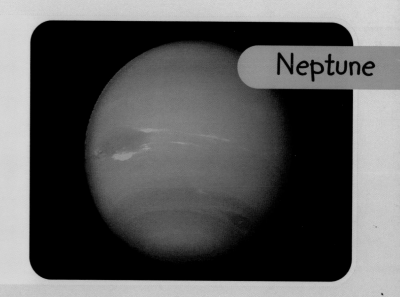

Neptune

Glossary

astronaut – a person who travels to space inside a spacecraft.

astronomer – a person who studies space, including the Sun, Moon, stars and planets.

planetoid – a planet-like object, smaller than the nine main planets in our solar system.

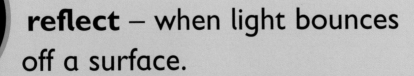

reflect – when light bounces off a surface.

Index

Carers' and teachers' notes

- Explain to your child that this book is non-fiction (i.e. that it provides facts and information rather than telling a story) and that it contains a contents page, a glossary and an index.
- Explain that by looking at the contents page, the reader can see what the book is about and the order in which the information appears in the book.
- Point out that the index is arranged alphabetically and can be used to locate specific information in the book.
- Explain that the glossary, also in alphabetical order, gives meanings for difficult or specialist words in the text.
- Re-read pages 4–5. Talk with your child about things that are hot and things that are cold. Use a radiator or some other heat source to show how quickly you lose the heat as you move away.
- Warn your child never to look directly at the sun as it can damage his/her eyes.
- Use a ball to show how the Earth moves slowly round on its axis.
- Encourage your child to look at the Moon each night to see its different stages.
- Together, sing 'Twinkle, Twinkle Little Star'.
- Count the planets in the diagram on pages 18–19. Repeat the names of the planets until your child is familiar with them. To help remember the names of the planets and their order from the Sun, make up a mnemonic, for example, **M**y **V**ery **E**asy **M**ethod **J**ust **S**et **U**p **N**ine **P**lanets.
- Together, use reference books or the Internet to find out a fact about each of the nine planets. Help your child to write down his/her facts.
- Help your child to write a fact sheet for an alien who wants to come and visit the Earth, explaining all about the planet. Encourage your child to draw pictures to accompany his/her text. Can your child draw the alien for whom the fact sheet is intended?